# Contents

The Publishers are grateful to the following for their
permission to reproduce photographs:-
Ardea for page 56; Jomo Kenyatta Foundation for page 20;
Picturepoint for page 44; Tanzania Information Services for
page 74.

We regret we are unable to trace the copyright holder of the
photograph on page 23 and would welcome any information
enabling us to do so.

Illustrated by Gay Galsworthy

First Published 1987
Third impression 1992

ISBN 0 582 58499 X

Published by Longman Group UK Limited
Longman House, Burnt Mill, Harlow,
Essex CM20 2JE, England

Produced by Longman Group (FE) Ltd.
Printed in Hong Kong

# Foreword

The improved Primary Science syllabus was revised and written by the National Primary Science Panel, National Curriculum Development Centre. This Basic Primary Science Course is written following this syllabus.

The Pupil's Books for this course will generate lively activities both inside and outside the classroom. These activities will help the pupils develop the curiosity and skills needed for scientific study. Therefore, I advise the pupils to ask questions, carry out observations and other activities and draw their own conclusions.

I wish to thank Mr D.S. Kiyimba, Primary Science Specialist, and Secretary to the Writing Panel for having worked so hard in the National Curriculum Development Centre to produce the Primary Science Course books for Uganda. We are also grateful for the help and support of our publishers, especially their consultant Mr R.J. Sayles.

Vincent E. Bua
Director
National Curriculum Development Centre
Ministry of Education

# To the pupil

The Basic Primary Science Course for Uganda is for pupils from Primary 1 to Primary 7. Its aim is not only to help you to pass your examinations, but also to help you to develop a scientific way of thinking and of doing things. It will help you to understand things around you and it will prepare you for education after Primary School. It will help you to gain scientific knowledge so that you can live a full and useful life. Therefore I encourage you to do all the activities and exercises in this book. The book is simple and you can use it even without your teacher.

Your teacher knows how much science you have to learn in Primary 5. He or she may teach you some things or ask you to do activities which are not in this book. Do them with pleasure.

David S. Kiyimba (Secretary)
Senior Science Specialist
National Curriculum Development Centre
Ministry of Education

# 1

# Bees

There are many different kinds of bees. Most bees are <u>solitary bees</u> that live alone. Others are <u>social bees</u> that live and work together in large groups. The most social bee of all is the <u>honey bee</u>.

Honey bees live together in groups of thousands of bees, called <u>colonies</u>. They may build their home in a box, a hollow tree or a bee hive.

Each colony has three types of bee:
1   the queen bee – she lays eggs. There is one mature queen in each colony.
2   the workers – they gather food and care for the young and make the greatest number in a colony.
3   the drones – they fertilise the queen.

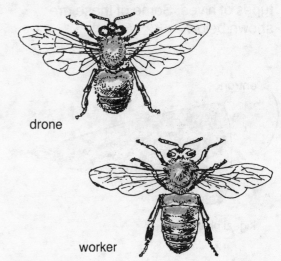

drone

worker

queen

## Exercises
1   Draw and name the three kinds of honey bee.
2   How does the queen bee look different from the other two?
3   Which bees are male?
4   Which bees do not have stings?
5   What is the main duty of the queen?
6   Which of these are in the greatest numbers? Why?
    i)   drones
    ii)  workers
    iii) queen

# Keeping bees

Thousands of years ago, people ate honey that they collected from the hives of wild bees. Some of these people learnt to make simple hives. They then had honey near their homes.

Today, people keep bees in different types of hives. Some of these are shown below.

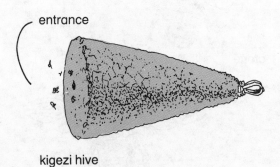

entrance

kigezi hive

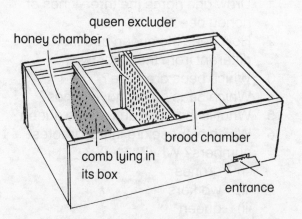

honey chamber

queen excluder

comb lying in its box

brood chamber

entrance

## Activities

1 Draw a traditional hive and a modern hive and name them.
2 Which kind of hive would you like to have? Why?
3 What materials would you use to make a simple traditional hive? If possible, visit a local beekeeper and talk with him about making hives.
4 Look at the comb shown below. Each cell contains honey or pollen. Sometimes cells contain eggs or developing bees.
Every cell has the same shape. How many sides does each cell have?
What is this shape called?

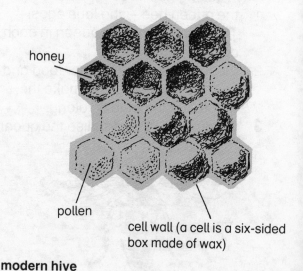

honey

pollen

cell wall (a cell is a six-sided box made of wax)

**modern hive**

# Life history of the bee

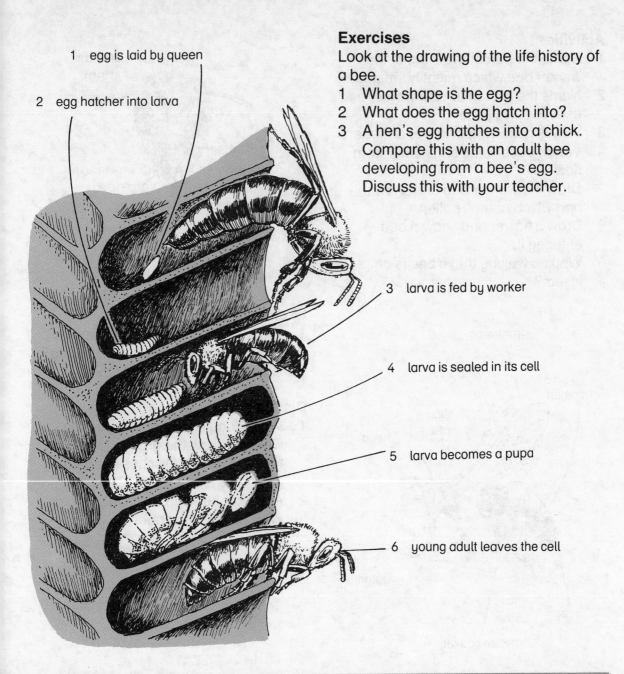

1    egg is laid by queen

2    egg hatcher into larva

3    larva is fed by worker

4    larva is sealed in its cell

5    larva becomes a pupa

6    young adult leaves the cell

**Exercises**

Look at the drawing of the life history of a bee.

1    What shape is the egg?

2    What does the egg hatch into?

3    A hen's egg hatches into a chick. Compare this with an adult bee developing from a bee's egg. Discuss this with your teacher.

# Parts of the honey bee

## Activities

1 Name the part of the body of the worker bee which might harm you.
2 Name the part which the worker bee uses to carry pollen.
3 Why is pollen important to a farmer?
4 Watch bees collecting nectar from flowers.
   Draw the worker bee and show the part which carries pollen.
5 Draw a flower and show a bee entering it.
6 Why do we say that a bee is an insect?

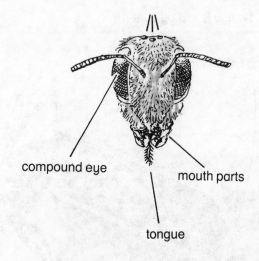

compound eye

mouth parts

tongue

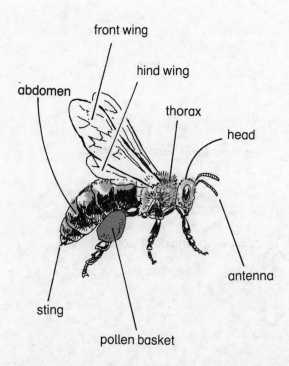

front wing

hind wing

abdomen

thorax

head

sting

pollen basket

antenna

## Exercises

1 What part of its body does the bee use to suck nectar, water or honey?
2 How is nectar important to us?

## Discussion questions

1 When food is in short supply, the workers allow the drones to starve to death. Why? Discuss this with your teacher.
2 A worker bee can sting only once. Why can't it sting again?

# 2

# Matter

In book 4 you learnt how to measure objects. You saw that objects always have <u>weight</u> and <u>volume</u>. We can find out the weight of an object by <u>weighing</u> it. The volume of an object is the space which it fills. That is, <u>objects occupy space</u>.

When you learnt about air you saw that air also occupies space (it has volume). Air has weight too. You may have weighed air.

> **Anything which has weight has mass also.**

## Density

Mass and volume help you to find the <u>densities</u> of different materials.

Some things are more dense than others. Think of a cube made of cork and a cube of exactly the same size made of stone.

Which weighs more?

Which has the greater mass?

Density depends upon mass and volume. To find the density of any object we divide the mass by the volume.

> $$\text{Density} = \frac{\text{mass}}{\text{volume}}$$

**Example**

Let us find the density of the cork and stone.

The mass of the cork is  1 gram (g).

The volume of the cork is  5 cubic centimetres (cm$^3$).

$$\text{Density is } \frac{\text{mass}}{\text{volume}} = \frac{1}{5}$$

Therefore the density of the cork is $\frac{1}{5}$ or 0.2 gram per cubic centimetre (g/cm$^3$).

The mass of the stone is  15 grams (g).

The volume of the stone is  5 cubic centimetres (cm$^3$).

$$\text{Density is } \frac{\text{mass}}{\text{volume}} = \frac{15}{5} = 3$$

Therefore the density of the stone is 3 grams per cubic centimetre (g/cm$^3$).

The stone is 15 times more dense than the cork.

**Exercise**

1   Look at the above example.
   Which has the greater density - cork
   or stone?
   Is cork more or less dense than
   stone?

2   Fill in this table.

| mass (g) | volume (cm$^3$) | density (g/cm$^3$) |
|----------|-----------------|--------------------|
| 28 | 7 | |
| 18 | 6 | |
| 24 | 4 | |

## Activity

Drop the following things into a bucket of water: cork, stone, pin, nail, match, coin, pencil.

Which float? Which sink?

What can you say about the density of each object?

> **A thing will float if it is made of something which is less dense than water.**
> **A thing will sink if it is made of something which is more dense than water.**

## Matter

Mass and volume are two <u>properties</u> of things around us. But things can have other properties as well. Let us find out what these are.

We can say that all the things around us are made up of matter. These things can be solid, liquid or gas and that it can be weighed and occupies space.

Words like 'things', 'objects', 'materials' or 'substances' are usually used when talking about matter.

## Activities

Collect these materials: cooking fat, ripe bananas, rubber, stones, pieces of metal, seeds, cassava, glass tumblers, soap, paraffin, water, dry moss, a ball, plastic jerry cans, a shoe, a book, air.

1   Sort the materials into sets which are:
    i)   soft
    ii)  hard
    iii) of regular shape
    iv)  solid
    v)   liquid.

2   Pick the odd one out of the following sets:
    i)   ripe bananas, milk, rain drops, paraffin
    ii)  glass, stones, metal, air
    iii) ball, stones, cassava, dry moss
    iv)  air, shoe, seeds, book.

In question 1, all the things you classified as soft or hard or of regular shape could be reclassified as solid. Solids have a shape of their own e.g. a book or cassava.

Liquids have no shape of their own. A liquid has to be in a container, so it has the shape of the container e.g. milk, water, tea.

A material which can not be held except in a container with a lid is called a gas e.g. air.

3 Group all the things listed in question 2 into three sets - solids, liquids and gases. You should find that everything will fit into these sets.

> **Matter can, therefore, be divided into solids, liquids or gases. We say that things around us are either solid, liquid or gaseous. They can also be mixtures of solid and liquid, solid and gas or liquid and gas.**

## States of matter

### Activities

1 Break a fresh egg. Pour the egg onto a metal plate and stand the plate over boiling water. (You could use a small saucepan.) Carefully observe what happens.

2 Put a small lump of cooking fat (or cow ghee) in a small saucepan. Put the pan on the fire and leave for some time. Heat gently. Take care not to leave the pan on the fire for too long. It can catch fire. Note what happens.

3 Put a few drops of water in a pan and put on the fire. Note what happens.

4 Hold a clean, dry plate about 20 cm above a pan containing boiling water. What do you see on the plate after several minutes?

5 Experiment and find out what happens when:
 i) dry wood is burnt – does it change into a liquid?
 ii) potatoes are roasted – do they become fresh on cooling?

Solid, liquid and gas are called the three states of matter. Some things can easily change from one state to another.

Water is an example. Ice is a solid which melts to water (a liquid). If this liquid is heated we can see water vapour rising into the air. Water vapour is like a gas. We say that the liquid evaporates to a vapour. (The vapour from boiling water is called steam.)

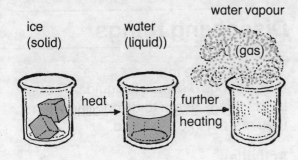

ice
(solid)
water
(liquid))
water vapour
(gas)

heat → further heating →

**Solid, liquid and gas are called
the three states of matter.**

It is easy to change water vapour back
to liquid water again. You just cool it.
We say that the water vapour (gas)
condenses to liquid water. If it becomes
very cold, the liquid water will freeze
to ice (solid). We say the liquid
solidifies to a solid.

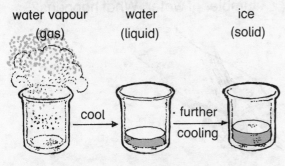

water vapour
(gas)
water
(liquid)
ice
(solid)

cool → further cooling →

Solid cooking fat is another substance
which easily changes state. If it is
heated it melts to hot, liquid cooking
fat. If this hot fat is cooled, it solidifies
to solid fat again. Many other
materials do not show these changes
of state so easily. This is the case
when wood is burnt. Cooling burnt
wood will not bring it back to its
original state.

**Solid, liquid and gas are called
the three states of matter.**

## Exercises

1 Give reasons why you think that
   light and sound are not made of
   matter.
2 Look at this list of objects. Pick out
   those which are not matter. Explain
   your choice in each case: air, wind,
   a river, rain drops, time, earth's
   atmosphere, thoughts, soil, trees.
3 Fill in the table below. Give
   examples of matter which are solids,
   liquids and gases.

| solids | liquids | gases |
|--------|---------|-------|
|        |         |       |
|        |         |       |
|        |         |       |
|        |         |       |

# Mixtures

Many of the substances around us are mixtures – that is they are two or more different things mixed together. Look at the table.

| substance | mixture of: |
| --- | --- |
| concrete block | sand and cement |
| porridge | flour and water |
| air | several different gases |

# Dissolving things

Some things <u>dissolve</u> in liquids. That is, the things <u>seem to disappear</u> when they are put into the liquid.

## Activities

1  Pour one small spoon of clean white sugar into a tumbler of water. Stir. What happens?
2  Put small pieces of soap into water. What happens?
3  Pour a little alcohol into a tumbler of water. What happens?
4  Pour a little cooking oil into a tumbler of water. What happens?

sugar (solute)

tumbler

water (solvent)

## Solutions

If a substance <u>seems to disappear</u> when it is put into a liquid we say that it is soluble in the liquid.

For example, sugar is soluble in water.
Salt is soluble in water.
Potassium permanganate is soluble in water.
Alcohol is soluble in water.

We say that these substances form <u>solutions</u> with water.
A solution is clear (you can see through it). It can be colourless (salt in water) or coloured (potassium permanganate or copper sulphate in water).

The colour is the same throughout the whole solution. Substances which dissolve to form solutions are called <u>solutes</u>.

The water or liquid in which the substances dissolve is called a <u>solvent</u>.

Some substances do not dissolve when put into a liquid. We say that they are not soluble.

For example, sand is not soluble in water.
Beans are not soluble in water.
Paraffin is not soluble in water.
Cooking oil is not soluble in water.
Milk is not soluble in water.

When paraffin is put into water you can see a clear dividing line between the paraffin and water. The paraffin has not dissolved in the water. Nor has it mixed with the water.
When milk is put into water you cannot see a clear dividing line between the milk and the water. The milk has not dissolved in the water but it has mixed with it.

stir

solution of sugar and water

the sugar dissolves in the water

## Exercises

1. Why do we say that water mixes with milk but does not dissolve in it?
2. Why do we say that salty water is a solution but soapy water is not?

# Particles: dispersion and dilution

## Dispersion

Watch the smoke rising from fires on calm evenings. Observe how it spreads.

Sometimes, in the morning, you can see thick white mist in valleys. Later it spreads and clears.

When the bell goes at break you leave your classroom. Then you spread around the school compound to play with friends.

When your teacher sprays a little insecticide at the front of the class, the smell soon reaches the back.

If there are birds resting in a tree, and you disturb them, they will fly off and spread in the air.

Smoke, mist, insecticide, and birds spread in the air. We say that they disperse in the air.

Put some sugar in a mug of water and stir it. If you taste the mixture you will find that the sweetness has spread. When sugar dissolves in water, we could say that it disperses into the water.

## Activities

1   Put a drop of fresh milk into a clean tumbler of water. Stir just a little. What happens?

2   Prepare some sap from leaves or flowers. Dark or red sap is better than milky sap. Put a drop of the sap in the centre of a piece of clean blotting paper. Let it spread and dry.

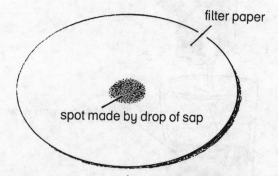

filter paper

spot made by drop of sap

Then, add a drop of clean water on the spot made by the sap. Let it spread over the spot. Add another drop of water and watch it spread.

Continue to add water, a drop at a time. Avoid making the paper too wet.
Note and draw what happens. Repeat, using alcohol instead of water.

3   Put clean water in a clear glass tumbler. Gently drop a crystal of potassium permanganate into the water, and leave for some time. Check on what is happening and note any changes.

4   Put a cube of wood in a similar tumbler of water and leave. Check on it and record what you see.

5   Put equal amounts of clean water into two glass tumblers.
    In one tumbler add a spoonful of uncrushed salt.
    In the other add an equal amount of crushed salt.
    Stir both glasses until the salt dissolves. How long does it take the salt to dissolve in each case?

These activities will show you that matter is sometimes capable of spreading. This is called <u>dispersion</u>.

Some things disperse well into others. Examples are smoke in air, milk in water, salt in water, potassium permanganate in water.

Some things disperse at first and then settle at the bottom of the container. Examples are maize flour in water, orange juice in water and soil in water.

Some things do not disperse into others. Wood does not spread in water. Sand does not spread in water, but settles to the bottom.

> **We say that dispersion is possible with materials which can easily break up into small particles.**

## Exercises

1   Why do you think that milk is able to spread in water? Discuss this with your teacher.

2   When water boils it gives off steam. This is visible just above the surface of the boiling water. It is not easily seen further away from the water. How do you explain this?

3   If somebody uses onions to fry food in one room, people in nearby rooms may be able to smell the cooking.
    How do you explain this?
    How far away would you smell the cooking?

# Separation of soil particles in water

Soil in water is an example of dispersion and settling.
Put two spoonfuls of soil into a large tumbler of water. What do you observe?
The particles of soil will disperse through the water. The heaviest particles will sink to the bottom. The lightest ones stay floating on the surface. Slightly dispersed heavier particles stay in the muddy water.

humus (floating remains of dead plant matter)

glass jar

cloudy water

clay

fine sand

coarse sand and small stones

# Is matter made of particles?

## Activities

1  i)  Sift some maize flour using a fine wire mesh (wire gauze will do). Put aside the residue (this is what will not pass through the mesh). Let the sifted flour fall on a piece of paper.

maize flour (flour that does not pass through the mesh is the first residue)

paper

fine gauze (first sieve)

sifted flour

ii)  Find a finer mesh and sift the flour that passed through the first mesh. Put aside the residue. Let the sifted flour fall on a clean cloth.

first residue (flour that does not pass through the mesh is the second residue)

finer gauze (second sieve)

clean cloth

sifted flour

iii)  Fold the cloth containing the flour to make a sifting cloth bag. Shake it to sift the flour and let the sifted flour fall on a piece of paper. Open up the cloth bag and spread the residue.

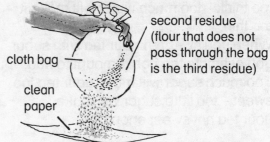

second residue (flour that does not pass through the bag is the third residue)

cloth bag

clean paper

iv)  Use a hand lens to examine the flour and residue at each stage. What do you see? How would you grade the flour if you were a maize miller?

2  Find a thin copper wire. Cut it into two equal parts with a pair of scissors. Cut each part again into two, and continue to halve each part until you can hold the wire no more. Discuss with your teacher what you would get if you were able to continue cutting the wire. Is it possible to make the wire whole again? How would you do it?

---

These activities show that matter can break up into <u>small bits</u>, or particles.
In some cases e.g. copper, these particles cannot be put together to form the grains.

# Dilution

When you make porridge you estimate the right amounts of flour to water. Too much flour and your porridge will be too thick – too much water will make it too thin.

When you sweeten your tea with sugar you estimate the right amount to add. Too much sugar will make your tea too sweet – too little sugar will make your tea not sweet enough.

## Exercises

1 Why do you stir sugar in your tea before drinking?
2 Why are people against buying milk which has had water added to it?

## Activities

1 Add one spoon of sugar to a cup of tea. Do not stir and leave to stand for twenty minutes. Has the sugar spread evenly throughout the tea?

2 Look at the diagram at the bottom of the page.
Put clean milk into a glass tumbler A. Get three more tumblers B, C and D, and clean drinking water in a mug. The tumblers should all be the same size and shape.

i) Pour half of the milk from A into B. Add water to B until it is full.
ii) Then pour half of B into C. Add water to C until it is full.
iii) Pour half of C into D. Add water to D until it is full. Then pour away half of D. You should be left with glasses A, B, C and D half-full. Only A contains milk without water.
iv) Put the glasses side by side. Look carefully at their contents and compare them.

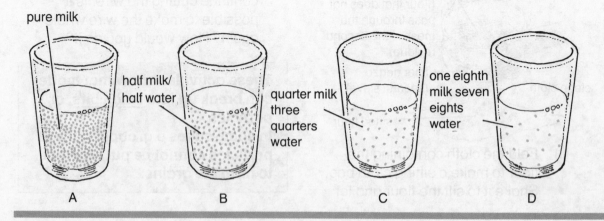

pure milk

half milk/ half water

quarter milk three quarters water

one eighth milk seven eights water

A      B      C      D

3 Do a similar experiment using maize flour in water instead of milk. Use a hand lens to examine the contents of the glasses.

4 Do a similar experiment, but in A put drinking water in which two teaspoons of sugar have been added. Use a teaspoon to taste the contents of each glass, starting with glass D.

Adding water to porridge makes the porridge thin. Adding water to milk makes it thin. Adding water to a sugar solution makes it less sweet. We say that the solution has been <u>diluted</u>.

In the above experiments, the contents of glass A were rich, or concentrated. The contents of glass D were thin or <u>dilute</u>.

Adding water to the contents of A to make solutions weaker is called <u>dilution</u>.

The words concentrated and dilute are used to describe solutions e.g. sugar in water or tea.

When describing other mixtures e.g. milk or porridge, other words can be used such as rich, thick, thin or light.

> **Dilution occurs because matter is made up of small particles. These can spread to all parts of the solution.**

Copper (II) sulphate and potassium (IV) permanganate make coloured solutions in water. When these solutions are diluted with more water, the colour gets fainter. Why do you think this happens? Discuss this with your teacher.

### Activities

1 You are given two solutions of copper (II) sulphate, S and R. How can you tell that S is more dilute than R?

2 You are given some salt and four glasses, A, B, C and D. Make a solution of salt in water, in glass A. Then pour half of A into B and fill B up with water.
Then pour half of B into C and fill C up with water.
Then pour half of C into D and fill D up with water.
You have now made four salt solutions of different concentrations. Get four tin lids and

fill one lid with A, one with B, one with C and one with D. Place the lids in a dry place where the air is moving. Look at the lids every two hours.

What is happening?

What remains in the lids after several days?

Discuss with your teacher why the solution in A is more concentrated than the solution in D.

3 Discuss with your teacher and set up an experiment to grow a crystal of copper II sulphate.

4 Look at cement blocks being made. What materials are used? How big are the particles of each material?

5 Your teacher will show you how to scrape off a little piece of metal using a file. Collect the metal on a clean piece of paper and examine the pieces.

6 Put a drop of cooking oil in a glass of water. What happens?

Touch the oily areas with a dry twig, poking many times at the surface. Then add a drop of soapy water. Stir or shake the glass slightly. Leave to settle. What happens?

7 Put some alcohol e.g. Uganda Waragi in a glass.

Add a piece of fat e.g. ghee, margarine, 'kimbo' or cooking oil. Cover the glass with a saucer (or your palm) and shake carefully. Leave to stand.

What happens?

# 3

# Work and energy

## Force

If you press an egg between your palms at the right place it breaks. If you kick a ball it moves. When a ripe fruit is squeezed it loses shape. You can move a bicycle by pushing or pedalling it. You can stretch a piece of rubber by pulling it (this also makes it change its shape).
You have probably done all these things. They involve pushing or pulling, or pressing or striking a blow.

## Exercises

1  If you push against a big tree it hardly shakes. But if you push against a small tree it may bend. Why?
2  There are five pupils in team A and five in team B. Each team says that it is the stronger. You have to test which is the stronger and you are given a rope and nothing else. How would you test the two teams?

## Activities

1  Take a rubber band. Hold it with both hands and stretch it.
   What do you feel?
   Let go with one hand. What happens?

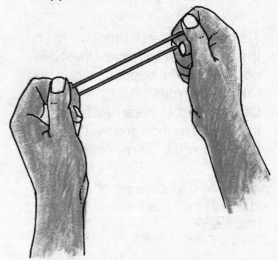

Repeat this several times.
Make sure you do not hurt yourself or your friends.

2   Wind a stretched rubber band on a
    smooth piece of wood.
    Release the rubber band at one
    end. What happens?

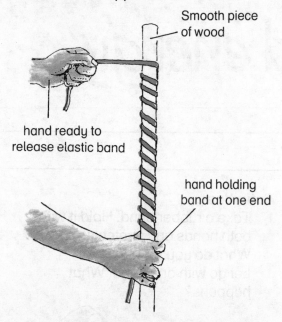

Smooth piece
of wood

hand ready to
release elastic band

hand holding
band at one end

3   Tie a rope on a tree branch. Pull on
    the free end of the rope. What do
    you feel? What happens when you
    release the rope?

4   Lift an object (a chair or a brick) off
    the floor. What do you feel? What
    happens when you release the
    object?

5   Squeeze a football which is well-
    inflated (well-filled with air). What do
    you feel?

These exercises and activities show
that pushing, lifting, stretching, pulling
and pressing things are not easy. The
objects <u>resist</u>. We have to 'try hard' to
make these things do what we want. We
have to '<u>force</u>' them.

Thus, a pull is a force. We say that
force must be used to pull things.
Force is also needed to push, press,
squeeze, lift, kick or cut. List some
other activities which need the use of
force.

## Activities

1 Place a ball on level ground. Kick it and note what happens.
2 Place a ball of soft clay on a table. Hit the ball sideways. What happens?
3 With both hands pull hard at a long piece of chalk. What happens? What would happen if you used a stick of soft clay instead?
Try to find out.

Your investigations should show that forces produce two types of results on objects:

1 the objects may move
2 the objects may change shape or break.

> **We say that when a force acts on an object the object may move. When things move we say they are in <u>motion</u>. Therefore, force causes motion.**

## Examples of forces

A tug-of-war is a game shown at the bottom of this page..

Each team pulls on a rope. When one team is stronger than the other, the weaker team is pulled along with the rope. The weaker team is moved towards the stronger team. What happens if the two teams are of equal strength?

When objects are pulled they move towards the force pulling them. When objects are pushed they move in the direction of the force pushing them.

> **When objects move they go in the direction of the force acting on them.**

force ← movement towards team A → force

team A                    team B

## Exercises

1   Describe what is happening in this picture. What would happen if the drum were much heavier?

2   What is happening here? What will happen if the goat pulls much harder?

Adults can lift things which are too heavy for a child. They can act with a bigger force. Discuss with your teacher why it is easier to lift a 10 kg bag of salt than a 50 kg bag?

## Friction

The weight of a log is 20 kg. You need a large force to lift the log but a smaller force to pull the log along the ground. If the surface below the log is smooth, then it is easy to pull the log. If the ground is rough then it is hard to pull the log.

When you try to lift the log, the weight of the log tries to stop you.

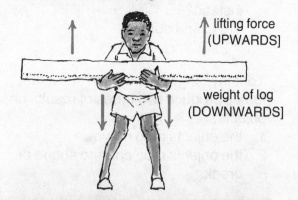

lifting force (UPWARDS)

weight of log (DOWNWARDS)

**Weight is a force. It is the force which opposes your lifting force.**

When you pull the log along the ground, your force is opposed by the resisting force of the rough ground. This is called <u>friction</u>.

## Exercises

1   Why do car tyres and the soles of your shoes become worn out with use?

2   Discuss with your teacher why objects don't float freely in the air.

# Motion

When you go to school you move from your home. You may walk or run to cover the distance. You could move the same distance by bicycle or bus or car. Car would be quicker than cycling, but cycling is quicker than walking. Animals move from place to place. Birds walk, jump or fly. Even the chameleon moves from one branch to another.

Chameleon

Trees do not move from place to place but the wind can shake and swing them. (Wind is moving air.)

Water flows in pipes and taps, in rivers and down sloping surfaces.

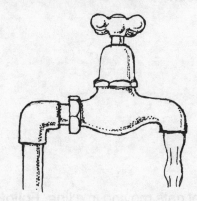

We have to push or pull or drive or roll other objects to move them. A force is needed to make things move. How could we make a ball move?

> **Moving objects are said to be in motion. Motion is the continuous activity of moving.**

## Exercises

1  List four things which you have seen in motion today.
2  What animal moves very slowly?
3  State four different things which move high above the earth's surface.
4  There are five birds – a dove, a crested crane, a crow, an eagle, and a vulture. Which flies fastest? Which is slowest?
5  Arrange these animals, beginning with the fastest:
   frog
   snal
   sheep
   dog
   chameleon
   cow
   ant

## Activities

1  Look at ants moving in a line. Follow the movement of one ant (an ant carrying a bit of food will be easier to follow). Estimate the distance moved by the ant in one minute.
2  Go to the nearest stream and watch the water flow. Drop some leaves in the water. What happens to them? Try to measure the distance travelled by the leaf in two minutes.

Measure how far the leaf goes in:
 i)   one minute
 ii)  one second

3  Get a friend to ride a bicycle on level ground. Ask him to unbutton his shirt before he rides.
   What happens to his shirt when he cycles quickly? Discuss what happens with your teacher.

Ask your friend to pedal for a little and then stop pedaling. If he does not use his brakes, will he stop in the end? Why?

Now ask your friend to ride a bicycle in a straight line and then to stop pedaling. If the brakes are not applied the bicycle should freewheel. Measure the distance travelled (after your friend has stopped pedaling) in half a minute. How far does your friend travel in one second?

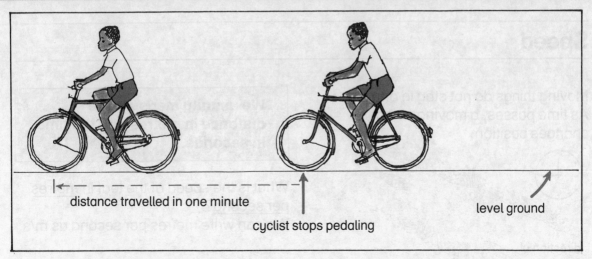

distance travelled in one minute

cyclist stops pedaling

level ground

Your friend had to pedal to start his bicycle moving. His legs gave the force needed to move the bicycle. Force is always needed to start motion.

When your friend was moving he felt a 'wind' blowing in his face. The 'wind' also blew out his shirt. The 'wind' is the resistance of the air. It helped to slow him down.

Your friend finally stopped without using brakes. This was due to the resistance of the air, and the resistance of the ground (friction) slowing down the wheels of his bicycle.

The wind and friction gave the force to stop his motion.

**Force is always needed to stop motion.**

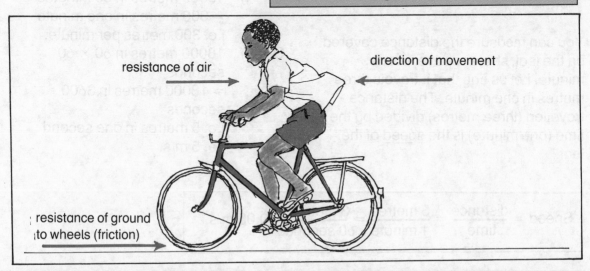

resistance of air

direction of movement

resistance of ground to wheels (friction)

# Speed

Moving things do not stay in one place. As time passes, a moving object changes position.

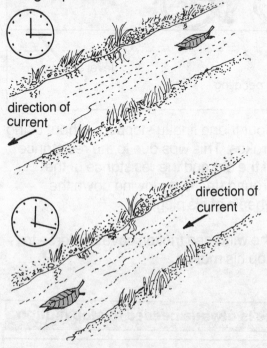

direction of current

direction of current

You can measure the distance covered by the leaf, shown above, in one minute. Let us say that it travels three metres in one minute. The distance travelled (three metres) divided by the time (one minute) is the speed of the leaf.

**We usually measure the distance in metres and the time in seconds.**

What is the speed of the leaf in metres per second?
We can write metres per second as m/s.

Sometimes we write speed as kilometres per hour or k/h. We can change this into metres per second:

18 km/h means 18 kilometres are travelled in one hour
or 18 × 1000 metres are travelled in 60 minutes
or 18 × 1000 metres are travelled in 60 × 60 seconds.
We can therefore write:

i)   18000 metres in 60 minutes
     = 300 metres in one minute
     i.e. 300 metres per minute.

Or ii)   18000 metres in 60 × 60 seconds
     = 18000 metres in 3600 seconds
     i.e. 5 metres in one second
     i.e. 5 m/s.

$$\text{Speed} = \frac{\text{distance}}{\text{time}} = \frac{3 \text{ metres}}{1 \text{ minute}} = \frac{3 \text{ metres}}{60 \text{ seconds}} = 0.05 \text{ m/s}$$

## Exercises

1  The speed of a rolling ball was 10 metres per second (10 m/s). What distance did it move in 3 seconds?

2  Fill in the gaps in the table below:

| distance moved (metres) | 8 | | 40 | 50 | 15 |
|---|---|---|---|---|---|
| speed of cyclist (m/s) | | 5 | 5 | | 10 |
| time taken (seconds) | 2 | 5 | | 20 | |

3  A car covers 50 kilometres in one hour. What is the speed of the car (in kilometres per hour)? How far will the car go in two hours?

# Different forms of work

Fetching water from a well is work. So is building a house or carrying fire wood. In each of these an object is lifted and moved to another place. A force is used to move these objects.

> **Whenever a force makes objects move, work is done.**

## Exercises

1  In which of the following activities is work done? Discuss this with your teacher.
   i) pushing a bicycle along the road
   ii) writing a letter with a pen
   iii) kicking a ball
   iv) sitting in a chair and thinking
   v) hammering a nail
   vi) sleeping.

2  Your parents ask you to fill a drum with water. They leave you the drum and a small bucket which holds 10 kg (10 litres). The drum holds 200 kg (200 litres). How would you do this task if the spring is downhill from your home?

## Activities

1  Push a heavy stone along the ground. Tie a rope around the stone and drag it along. What does it feel like in each case?
2  Lift the stone and carry it up some stairs or a slope. (Put it down before you feel too tired.)
   Is this more difficult than pushing or dragging the stone?

Doing work makes a person tired. He or she may sweat and breathe more heavily, or need to rest when working. Sometimes work must be done a little bit at a time. It is easy to draw 10 kg of water at a time. 200 kg would be too heavy but 10 kg can be drawn twenty times.

We have said that work is done when a force makes objects move. Writing is work. The pen moves across the page. A force is needed to move the pen. Where does the force come from?

## Activities

1  Write your name across two lines of your page. Now write across four lines of your page.
   Did you do more work in writing two or four lines?

2  Carry a stone up five steps. Now carry the same stone up ten steps. When did you do more work? Which made you feel more tired?

The greater the distance moved by the force, the greater the work done. When you carry a stone up ten stairs you do twice as much work as when you carry it up five stairs. But you used the same amount of force to carry the stone.
We can say:

**Work done = force × distance moved**

# Energy

A sick person feels weak. He or she cannot carry loads easily. He or she cannot exert enough force.
A baby cannot do heavy work. Nor can a hungry person. Why not?
To do heavy work a big force is needed. A strong person can exert a large force. He or she can easily lift, carry, pull or kick things.

To exert a force a person needs energy. A strong person has lots of energy. He can do plenty of work. A sick person has little energy. He should not do heavy work.

| If you have energy you can do work. |
|---|

# Types of energy

There are many different types of energy.

## Kinetic energy

Moving things have kinetic energy. All things that move have kinetic energy, but only while they are moving. A stationary car does not have kinetic energy. A moving car does.

### Exercises

1   Pick from the following, those objects or people which have kinetic energy?
   i)   a girl running along a road
   ii)  a car travelling at 30 km per hour
   iii) a car standing still at traffic lights
   iv) a man sleeping in a chair
   v)  an arrow flying through the air
   vi) a brick dropping from a wall.
2   When do you have kinetic energy?

| Kinetic energy is the energy of moving things. |
|---|

## Potential energy

Moving things have kinetic energy but stationary things can also have energy. Imagine that you are sitting quite still in a chair.

Are you doing work?

Have you got kinetic energy?

Although you are not moving you still have a form of energy. It is called potential energy.

Potential energy is the energy that is stored up inside you.

this man is standing still but he has potential energy

### Exercise

Do you have potential energy or kinetic energy when you are:

i)   running home from school
ii)  sitting still and listening to the teacher
iii) asleep
iv)  riding a bicycle
v)   building a wall?

When the man moves (lifts the bricks) he changes the potential energy which is stored inside his body into kinetic energy.

### Think of a man building a wall

What does he have to do? He has to lift bricks. Energy is needed to lift bricks. The energy comes from the man. The man has energy even when he is still. It is potential energy.

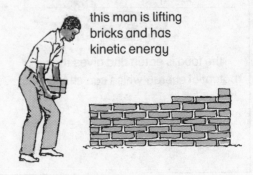

this man is lifting bricks and has kinetic energy

**Potential energy is energy which is there even when we are not using it.**

**One type of energy can change into another.**

Where does the potential energy of the man come from?
It comes from food. Food gives us energy. People who do not have food have little energy. They become weak and may die. The energy in food is called chemical energy. It is a type of potential energy.

When you eat well, your body has more energy. You become strong. You can run fast and throw spears or balls at high speeds. This is kinetic energy. Food also gives you heat energy which keeps you warm.

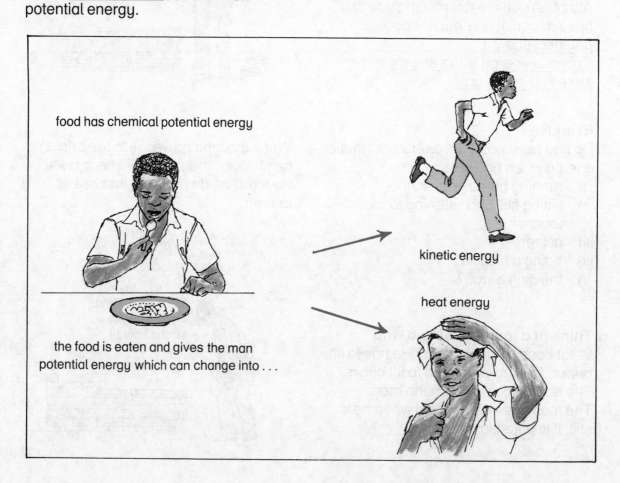

food has chemical potential energy

kinetic energy

heat energy

the food is eaten and gives the man potential energy which can change into . . .

We have seen that humans have potential energy. Non-living things can also have potential energy.

## Activity

Place a sweet potato on the floor and hold a pair of compasses about half a metre above the potato.

Drop the compasses onto the potato. Has it made a hole? Cut open the potato to find how deep the hole is. Repeat the experiment, this time dropping the compasses from a height of one metre. Is the hole deeper?

**Where has the energy come from to make a hole in the potato?**

It has come from the kinetic energy of the falling compasses.

Before the compasses fell, they had no kinetic energy. But they did have potential energy.

**Objects can have potential energy depending upon their position.**

The higher an object, the greater its potential energy. Therefore the higher an object, the more damage it does when it falls. That is why the compasses made a bigger hole when they were dropped from one metre.

## Exercises

1   Look at the picture.

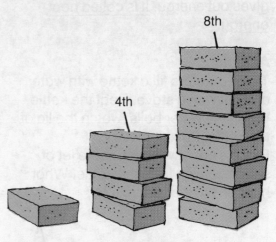

Which brick has the greatest potential energy?

Which has no potential energy?

Do any of the bricks have kinetic energy?

2   Fill in the missing words.

A man stood in a field. He stood quite still but he still had _____ energy. Then he started to build a brick wall. When he lifted the bricks he had _____ energy. The bricks lying on the ground had no _____ energy. But when the bricks were built high into the wall they had _____ energy. The higher the bricks, the more _____ energy they had.

The wall stood for many years. One windy day a brick fell from the wall. While it was falling it had _____ energy. It fell on top of a boy walking to school. . . . . .

# Heat energy

If you sit near a fire you get hot. The fire gives out energy. It is called heat energy.

## Activity

Three quarters fill a kettle with water and put it on a stove. Heat the kettle. When the water boils, watch the lid of the kettle. Does it move?

Place a paper windmill in the jet of steam coming from the kettle. What happens to the windmill?

Some kind of energy must be raising the kettle lid and turning the windmill. It is kinetic energy. The heat energy changes to kinetic energy of the steam. Where does it come from?

> **Heat energy can make things move.**

You will learn more about heat in chapter 5.

## Exercises

1 List five things which give us heat energy.

2 On a cold night you need a good blanket to keep yourself warm. Does this warmth come from:
   i)   the blanket
   ii)  the mattress
   iii) your body?
   Discuss this with your teacher.

# Light energy

The flame of a paraffin lamp gives out heat and light.

Light is a form of energy. Heat and light are often given out by the same source.

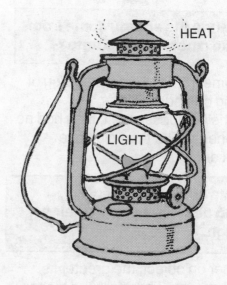

HEAT

LIGHT

### Exercises

1 What gives heat and light to our planet?
2 Write down five sources of light.

## Electrical energy

For question 2, did you list an electric light? We get light and heat from electricity.
Electricity is used in electric motors to lift objects or turn them.
Electricity is a type of energy.

## Magnetic energy

Another type of energy is magnetic energy. You will learn more about magnets in chapter 12.

## Sound energy

### Activity

1 Get a drum and beat it.
What do you hear?
Now put a coin on the skin of the drum. Beat the drum again and watch the coin. Does it move?

2 Heat some water in a kettle – until it boils. Listen to the kettle. Does it make a sound?

In the two activities above a sound is made.
What kind of energy is used to produce a sound from the drum?
What produces the sound from the kettle?

> **Sound is a form of energy.**

# Summary

1 The main forms of energy are:

> **kinetic**
> **potential**
> **chemical**
> heat
> light
> electric
> magnetic
> sound

2 One type of energy can change into another.

3 The sun is the main source of energy for our planet (earth). It gives us heat and light.
The sun helps plants to make food. Food is the main source of energy for our bodies. Animals (including us) get energy by eating plants or animals.
Plants get their energy from the heat and light of the sun.

**All of the energy in our body comes from the sun.**

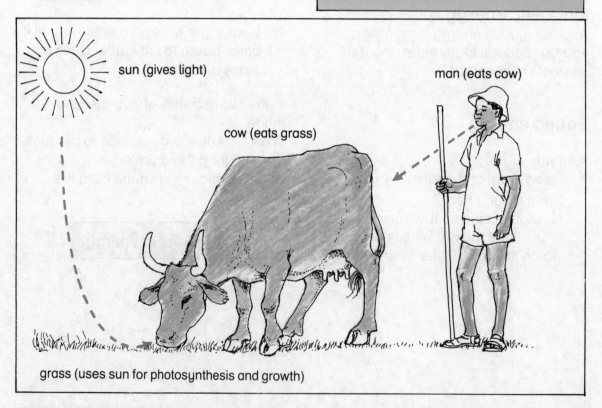

sun (gives light)

man (eats cow)

cow (eats grass)

grass (uses sun for photosynthesis and growth)

# 4
# Poultry

You learnt about poultry in Pupil's Book 4. Here is some more information.

## How to keep young chicks

Young chicks catch cold very easily, so must be kept warm. They need a special house or <u>brooder</u> for the first 3 – 4 weeks, and a constant supply of food and water.

A brooder should be warmed up before chicks are put in it. You can use a small charcoal stove (sigiri) or hurricane lamp or electricity as a source of heat. Check regularly that the room is not getting too hot or too cold.

Ventilation is important. Why? Brooders should have a ventilator but not too much draught. It is important that the brooder should be built at least 20 metres from the adult hen house. Why?

### Exercise
If one square metre is enough for sixteen chicks, how much space is needed by forty eight chicks?

### Activity
Make a brooder for fifty chicks.

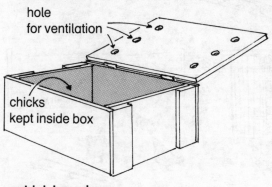

**a chick brooder**

**inside a brooder**

# Systems of poultry keeping

There are three main methods of keeping poultry. They are drawn below.

**deep litter system**
deep litter of straw or wood shavings

**battery system**   there are two birds per cage in this system

**free range system**

## Exercises

1 Discuss these methods with your teacher. What are the advantages and disadvantages of each system?
2 When looking after hens what sort of records should you keep and why?

# Feeding

Chicks should have a continuous supply of water and feed. Some apparatus for feeding chicks and chickens is shown below. You could make ones like these.

# 5
# Heat (energy)

Heat is a form of energy.
If something is hot it has heat energy.
List seven things which have heat
energy.

## Activity
Take two bowls and fill one with hot
water (do not use very hot water – you
will scald yourself). Put very cold water
in the other.

Stand for half a minute with one hand in
the hot water and the other in the cold
water.

Now remove both hands and plunge
them into a third bowl of warm water.
What does the warm water feel like to
your hand which has been in cold
water?
Do you get the same feeling in both
hands?

hot     warm     cold

# Temperature

| **Temperature is how hot or cold something is.** |
| --- |

We have talked about temperature in Pupil's Book 4.

Are hands suitable for measuring temperature?
How would you accurately measure temperature?

## Is temperature the same as heat?

### Activity
Take two kettles of equal size and fill one completely with water. Half-fill the other one. Place each kettle over a primus stove and heat for three minutes. You should heat each kettle for the same amount of time.
Then take the kettles away from the heat. Measure the temperature of the water in each kettle. How did you do this?
Which kettle has the hotter water? Why?
Are heat and temperature the same? Discuss and give reasons.

### Exercises
1   Name a natural source of heat.
2   Name six artificial sources of heat.
3   Give two examples where heat is useful to you.

41

# How do things change when heated?

## Change of state

### Activities
1   Get some wax or fat. Put it in a frying pan and heat it on a primus or charcoal stove. What happens?
2   Light a candle and hold it downwards. Hold a dish beneath the candle. What collects in the dish?

3   Heat water in a kettle until it boils. How do you know when it boils? Describe what you see.

## Expansion of solids

### Activities
1   Get a nail and make a hole in a tin can so that the nail fits tightly in the hole. Hold the nail with a pair of tongs. Heat the nail carefully in the flame of a primus stove for three minutes. Try to place the heated nail into the hole again (still holding the nail with the tongs). Does the nail fit the hole? What has happened? Discuss this with your teacher.
Let the nail cool down. Does it fit the hole now?

2   Tightly fix a thin metal wire in a wooden frame. Heat the wire with two candles.
What happens to the wire?
Let the wire cool. What happens?

3   Go outside early in the morning and draw the electricity or telephone wires. Draw them again at midday. The pictures below show the same set of wires at noon and in the evening. Which picture shows noon? Which picture shows evening? How can you tell this?

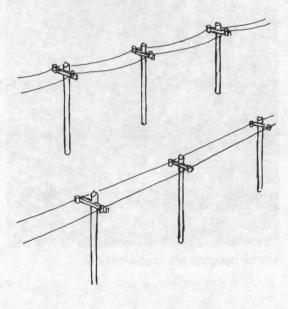

## Expansion of liquids

### Activity

1   Colour some water with ink and put some of the coloured water in an empty ink bottle. Put a cork, with a hole in it, in the mouth of the ink bottle. Pass a Bic Biro tube into the coloured water. Mark the level of the liquid in the Biro tube.
Now put the ink bottle into a tumbler of hot water and leave for five minutes.
What happens to the level of water in the tube?

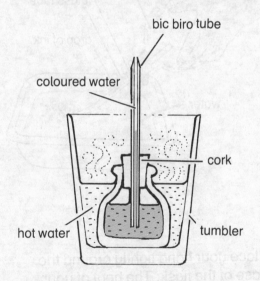

bic biro tube

coloured water

cork

hot water

tumbler

**These activities show that when metals are heated they <u>expand</u> (get bigger). When cooled they <u>contract</u> (get smaller).**

**This activity shows that liquids expand on heating. Expansion of liquids is used in thermometers.**

# Expansion of gases

**This activity shows that gases expand when heated.**

## Activity

Take a flask (or small bottle) and put a cork in the mouth of the flask. Make a hole in the cork. Pass a thin glass tube (or bic biro tube) through the hole. Now hold the flask by its bottom so that the end of the glass tube is in a tub of water.

What gas is expanding here?

Hot air balloons are filled with gas.

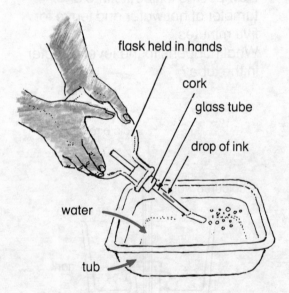

flask held in hands

cork

glass tube

drop of ink

water

tub

Place your hand tightly around the base of the flask. The heat of your hands will warm the air inside the flask.
What happens at the end of the glass tube?

# How does heat travel?

## Conduction

### Activity

Take some metal rods and fix a blob of candle wax 15 cm from the end of each rod. Each rod is of a different metal. Now place the rods as in the diagram. Heat the ends of the rods equally using a candle flame.

Watch the wax on the rods. What happens?

List the order of melting of the wax.

Now repeat the experiment using rods made of non-metals e.g. wood, glass or plastic.

How long does the wax take to melt for each rod?

Does wax melt more quickly on metals or on non-metals?

Why is the wax melting?

Where does the heat for melting the wax come from?

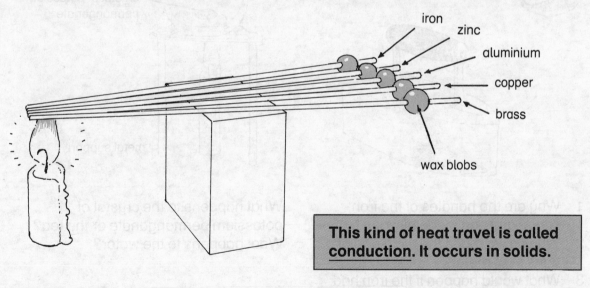

iron
zinc
aluminium
copper
brass
wax blobs

> **This kind of heat travel is called conduction. It occurs in solids.**

The heat from the flame travels up the rod. The rod conducts the heat. Some materials, like metals, conduct heat well. Others do not conduct heat well and are called insulators.

## Exercise

Look at the drawings and answer the questions below.

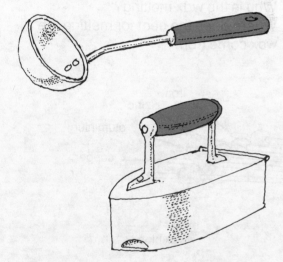

1   Why are the handles of the iron, spoon and pan made of wood?
2   Why do we make the main part of pans from metal?
3   What would happen if the iron had an iron handle?
4   What else could you use for making a pan handle?

## Convection

### Activity

Take a jam jar a fill it with water. Drop a crystal of potassium permanganate or a small tea bag to the bottom. Then heat the bottom of the jar with a candle very gently.

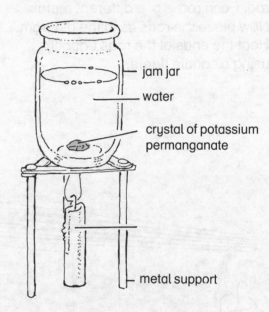

jam jar
water
crystal of potassium permanganate
metal support

What happens to the crystal of potassium permanganate or the tea? What happens to the water?

The heat energy from the candle is making the water move. This movement is shown up clearly by the purple dye of the potassium permanganate or brown dye from the tea.

> **This kind of heat travel is called <u>convection</u>. It occurs in liquids and gases.**

The water nearest to the candle (at the bottom of the tumbler) has heat energy. This makes it rise, so cooler water from above falls down to fill its place. This water is then warmed and rises.

We say that a <u>convection current</u> has been set up.

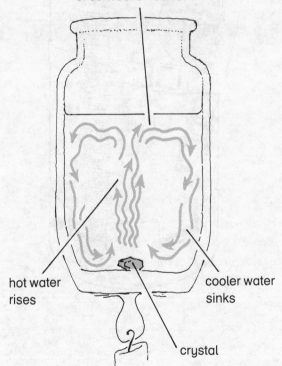

heat arrow showing direction of convection current

hot water rises

cooler water sinks

crystal

## Radiation

### Activities

1   Light a candle and hold your hands about 20 cm away from it. Hold your hands on either side of the candle. What do you feel as you bring your hands closer?

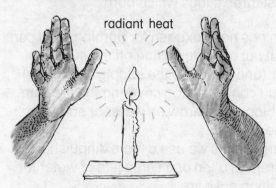

radiant heat

> **This kind of heat travel is called <u>radiation</u>. It occurs in gases.**

The heat <u>radiates</u> from the candle through the air. The <u>radiant heat</u> is strongest close to the candle.

2   Ask a friend to run around the compound to make him hot. Then hold the back of your hand close to his face. What do you feel?

Your friend's face also gave out radiant heat. You could feel it when you put your hand close to him.
The sun gives out radiant heat.
What else does?

# Burning

You may remember from Pupil's Book 4 that heat can cause burning. Some things burn when heated and some do not.

List three things which burn.

Things need oxygen for burning. You can put out a fire by cutting off the supply of air (and therefore the supply of oxygen). You can do this by covering the fire with a blanket or throwing water or sand on the flames.
Sometimes we use a fire extinguisher. Firemen often use fierce jets of water for putting out a fire.

# Summary of work on heat

**Exercise**

Fill in the missing words.

Heat is a form of _____ . The _____ is our main source of heat.

Without it there would be no life on earth.

Heat can cause materials (solids, liquids and gases) to _____ .

_____ causes a change of _____ .

Heat travels in three ways. These are _____ , _____ , and _____ .

# 6

# Domestic animals

The drawing below and opposite shows types of animals commonly found in Uganda.

**typical sheep**

upturned tail

long thick tail which hangs down

**typical goat**

large white

## Exercises

Look at the pictures while answering the questions.

1   Do all these animals suckle their young ones?
2   What does each animal feed on?
3   List these animals whose food consists:
    i)   entirely of plants or plant products
    ii)  of both animal and plant products.
4   Count the teats on one side of the large black pig. Count the teats on the goat.
     Which animal (pig or goat) gives birth to a greater number of babies?
5   Talk to farmers about their animals. Which animal will bring in most money?
6   Why do we keep goats, pigs and sheep?

landrace

# Goats and sheep

In Uganda, goats and sheep are reared for their meat. They do not produce much milk and do not raise as much money as pigs, poultry and cattle.

They are very resistent to disease. The most common diseases are internal worms and diarrhoea.

They can be kept in a house or outside. Below is a picture of a goat or sheep house.

You can rear these together in the same house or grazing area.

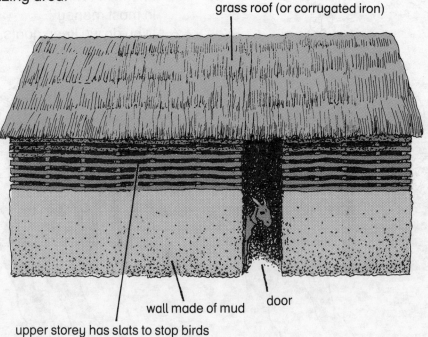

grass roof (or corrugated iron)

wall made of mud

door

upper storey has slats to stop birds

# Pigs

Pigs are reared for their meat which is called pork. Bacon and ham are different types of pig meat. Lard is pig fat. You can make sausages from pig meat.
The two most common breeds in Uganda are the Landrace and Large White.

## Looking after pigs
Pigs can be reared on pastures or in houses (often called styes). It is most common to rear them in houses. This is because not much land is needed and it is easy to control many pigs. Also, diseases such as worms can be controlled easily.

The two different systems of pig management are called extensive and intensive. <u>Extensive</u> systems provide temporary shelters but the pigs are on the pasture for most of the time. <u>Intensive</u> systems involve raising all the pigs indoors.

When building a pig house you should make sure that the floor is made firm with concrete. The walls can be made from blocks, bricks or hard timber. The roof should not leak and should protect the pigs from rain and too much sun. There should be a trough for food and water.

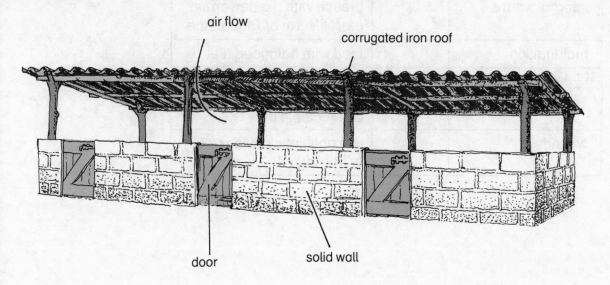

air flow

corrugated iron roof

door

solid wall

Pigs can feed on the same type of food as humans (they eat both animal and plant remains). Piglets are weaned at about eight weeks.

A sow should have two litters a year with ten to fourteen piglets per litter. A farrowing pen helps to stop the mother from crushing her babies.

## Activities

Visit a pig farm near your school and see what kinds of pigs they have there.

1　At what age does a sow mature?
2　Ask your teacher to help you to fill in the table below.

## Diseases in pigs and their control

| disease | signs | prevention & treatment |
|---|---|---|
| internal worms | | drench with pig dewormer, e.g. Nilverm or Pigerazine |
| malnutrition | | feed with balanced diet |
| piglet anaemia | | use red soil (sterilised), e.g. ant-hill soil or injectable iron |
| wounds | | use antibiotic powder or healing oil |

# 7

# Crop husbandry

## The school garden

The land surrounding your school can be useful if well planned and well looked after.
Look at the map below. What kind of activities are carried out here? If you have a school garden, look round it and see how it is planned.

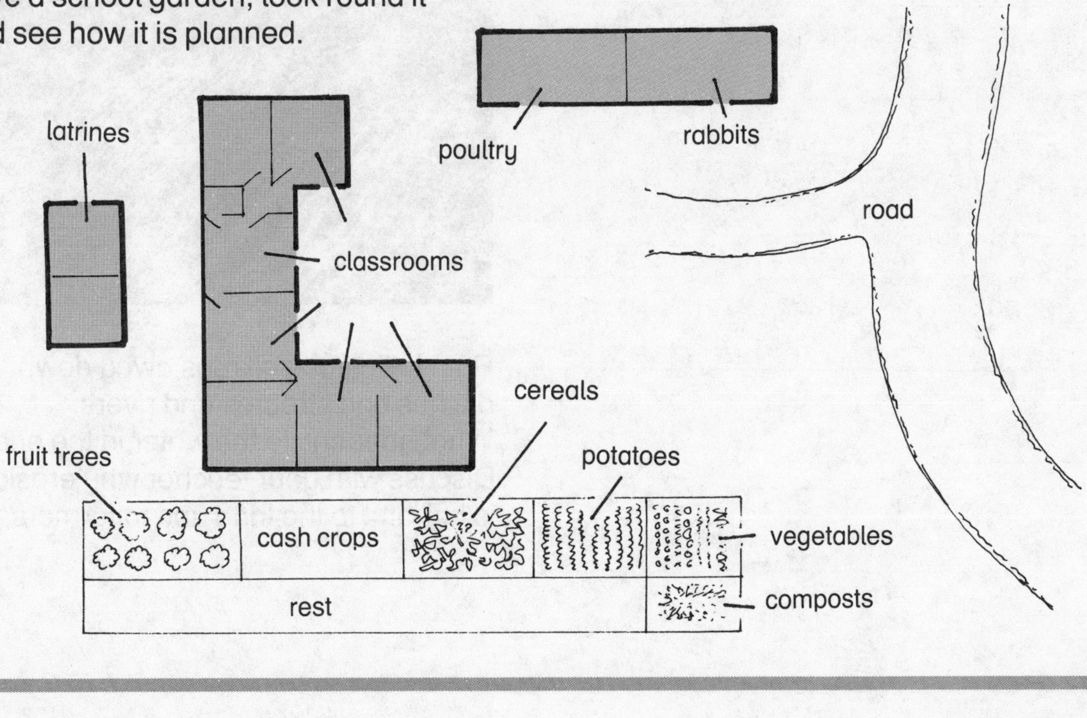

latrines

poultry    rabbits

road

classrooms

fruit trees

cereals

potatoes

cash crops

vegetables

compists

rest

## Exercises

1 Why is a school garden important?
2 Name crops which you might grow in a school garden.

## Planning a school garden

When planning a school garden you should think about several things.

1 The garden should be near the school.
2 It should be within a fence or hedge. Why?
3 There should be a number of spaced shade trees. Why?
4 Roads and paths should be well planned.
5 Much of the ground should be planted with grass.

# Soil erosion

When you come to school on a rainy day what do you notice? The rain falls onto the ground and there are puddles on the paths and roads. Sometimes roads turn into streams because water has run off the land. What colour is this water? What makes the water this colour?

We say that heavy rain falling on the land washes away or <u>erodes</u> the soil. Heavy rain causes <u>soil erosion</u>. The picture below shows you the action of water on the soil. Describe what is happening in the picture.

Rain falling on soil runs away down ditches and streams and rivers.
What happens to the water in the end?
Discuss with your teacher why erosion is harmful to the land and to farmers.

# How can we stop soil erosion?

One way is by terracing. The picture below shows crops of potatoes being grown on terraces.

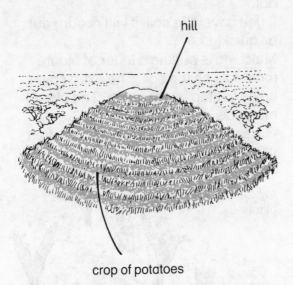

hill

crop of potatoes

soil ridge covered with grass

Terracing is used on steep land where heavy rain washes away the ground. Terracing is cutting steps in a slope. The flat part of each step is called a terrace.
Grass is planted along the edge of the terrace. Why?
Grass is very important in helping to stop erosion. Whenever land is too steep for cultivation it should be planted with grass.

What happens to soil if grass disappears? Why is it important that cattle should not overgraze the land?

## Activity

Your teacher will help you with this experiment on soil erosion.
Make two wooden boxes. They should have three short sides and one tall side.

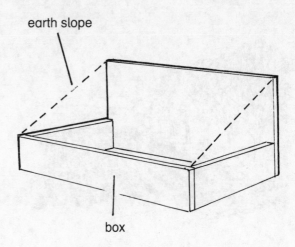

earth slope

box

Now pack each box with soil and build a slope against the high wall.
In the first box, lay a square of grass against the slope. Leave the other box bare.
Now trickle water down each slope and collect the water as it runs off.
Describe the appearance of the water in each case. Which water is more muddy? Why?

> **Growing plants on soil helps to stop soil erosion.**

Another way of stopping erosion is by growing trees. Tree roots bind the soil together. This stops the soil from being washed away.

Trees also act as <u>wind breaks</u>.

Discuss with your teacher how wind can cause soil erosion.

Land which is flat and surrounded by higher land soon becomes flooded. Therefore land at the bottom of a valley needs to be well drained.

### Exercises

1  What causes soil erosion?
2  How can you prevent soil erosion?

### Activity

If you live on a farm, see if soil erosion is happening there. Describe what you see.

> **Fast moving water and wind can cause soil erosion.**

# Feeding plants

## Mulching

What happens to soil when the hot sun shines on it? Does it take long to dry out.

If you cover the soil, it will not dry out as quickly.

<u>Mulching</u> is putting a layer of plant materials on the soil. The extra cover helps to stop evaporation. The plant materials are called <u>mulches</u>.

Grass or old banana leaves are often used as a mulch.

rows of young banana plants

mulch between rows

> **Mulching also helps to stop soil erosion.**

Why?

Discuss with your teacher other benefits of mulching.

**Activity**
If you have a school garden see if mulching is done there. Perhaps you could help with mulching.

## Compost

Compost is a mixture of animal and plant materials from the garden and farm. Animal waste, green plants and garden soil all make up a compost heap. It is a good fertiliser.

You make compost by piling animal and plant waste in a box or pit until full. Then add soil or cover with leaves and leave for a month.
The compost should be kept moist but not too wet.
After a month, turn the compost over. When it is ready it has the colour and texture of the best garden loam.

Remember, that different things take different times to rot down. Woody bits may take a long time so should not be added.

> **Compost is a very good fertiliser for the garden. It is very rich in nutrients.**

Find out why.
Discuss with your teacher what is happening in a compost heap.

**Activity**
Make a compost heap in your school garden. How long does it take your compost to form?

## Other types of fertiliser

If you visit a farm or your District Farm Institute, you will find that many different types of fertiliser are used.
1  Farmyard manure is made from the excreta of farm animals.
2  Green manure is made by burying leafy plant remains in the soil to form humus. Peas, beans and other vegetable crops rot down easily to form humus.
3  Animal remains are used to make fertiliser. These include dried blood, and hooves and horns (ground up).
4  Artificial fertilisers can be bought but are expensive. They are made from chemicals. You may see some of them at the Agricultural Shop or D.F.I. (District Farm Institute).

# Types of crops

Farmers grow many different kinds of crops.

Name the crops shown below.

Which of these do you grow at home or in the school garden? Go into the school garden and see how they are grown. How do we harvest and store the root crops shown here?

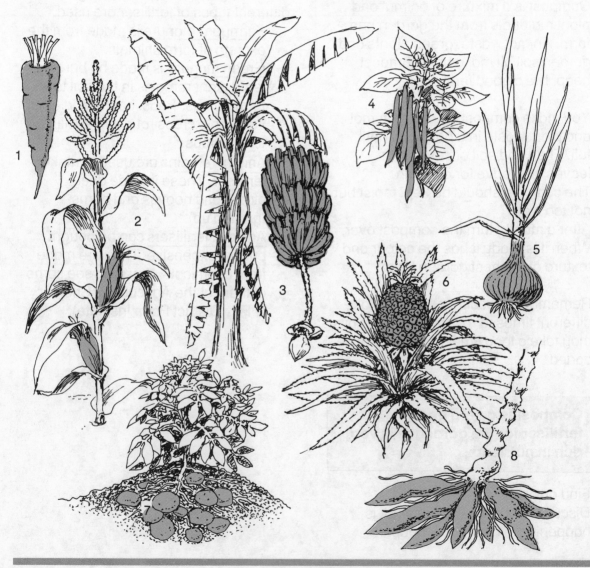

# Common pests and diseases of root crops

A pest is any animal which damages crops or livestock. Mammals, birds and insects can all be pests.

Below are some of the most common pests of root crops and how to control them.

Remember, that many chemical pesticides are poisonous to you and plants.

You must take care while handling them. Follow instructions carefully.

The diseases attacking root crops are mostly viruses. Control is mainly by destroying or treating those crops which have been attacked.

## Activity

Look around your school garden and check for pests and diseases.

Draw the pests. Which are the most common?

Set about controlling them.

(Remember to be careful with pesticides.)

| pests | control |
|---|---|
| | |
| | Dust the stems with Dieldrin. |
| | |
| | |
| | Shake off plants and kill by beating. Destroy plants which have been attacked or spray with Dieldrin. |
| | |

# 8

# Sound

Sound is a form of energy. We hear sound with our ears.

## Activities

1 Put a ruler on the edge of a desk and hold it firmly under a book. Press the ruler down and let it go suddenly.
What can you see? What can you hear? How can you vary the sound (note) made by the vibrating ruler?

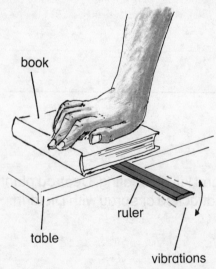

book

table

ruler

vibrations

2 Get a tin and take the lid off. Put a rubber band around the tin as shown in the diagram.

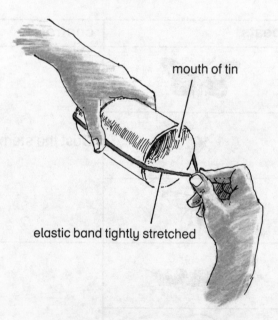

mouth of tin

elastic band tightly stretched

Pull the rubber band and let it go suddenly. What can you hear?

3 Put a rubber band over your thumb and finger. Pluck the rubber band.

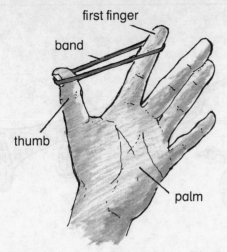

first finger

band

thumb

palm

What can you hear? What happens to the band?

4 Make a bow from a piece of springy wood and some string.

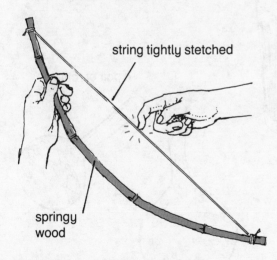

string tightly stetched

springy wood

Pluck the string. What happens?

5 Get two short metal bars. Put one on the table. Use the other to hit the bar on the table.

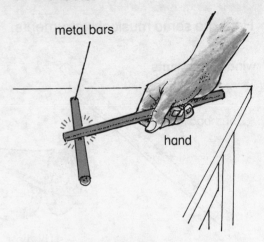

metal bars

hand

What do you hear?

6 Try hitting different objects. What noise do you make? What noise do you make when you hit a drum?

**Sound energy is made by vibration.**

# Musical instruments

Here are some musical instruments.

**wind instruments**

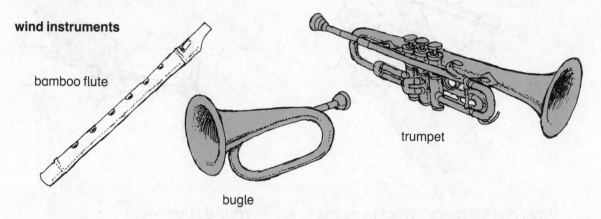

bamboo flute

bugle

trumpet

**percussion instruments**

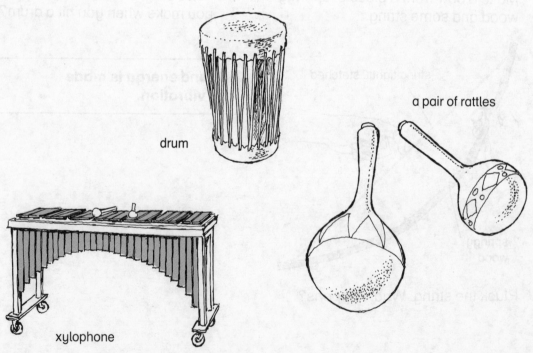

drum

a pair of rattles

xylophone

How is the sound made in each of these? Try and bring some of these instruments to school. Make sounds with them.

**string instruments**

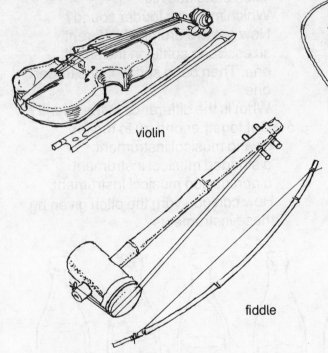

violin

fiddle

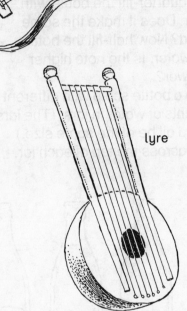

guitar

lyre

Below are some more instruments which you could make.

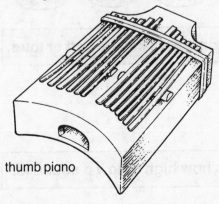

thumb piano

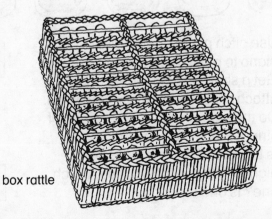

box rattle

# Loudness of sound and pitch

## Activities

1 Blow hard across the top of an empty bottle. Can you make a sound?
Now quarter-fill the bottle with water. Does it make the same sound? Now half-fill the bottle with water. Is the note higher or lower?

2 Make a bottle scale with different amounts of water in jars. (The jars should all be of the same size.) Blow across the top of each jar.

5 Take a drum and bang gently on it. Then bang heavily.
Which makes a louder sound?
Now get two drums of different sizes. Bang softly on the small one. Then bang softly on the larger one.
What is the difference in the sound?

6 Get together and try to make:
a wind musical instrument
a stringed musical instrument
a percussion musical instrument.
How can you vary the pitch given by these instruments?

3 Use pitch pipes or an African thumb piano to make high and low sounds.

4 Get a short piece of string and attach it to a piece of springy wood. Do the same with a longer piece of string. Pluck the two strings. Is the sound the same? Is one higher than the other? If so, which one? Is one louder?

**The same note can be soft or loud.**

**Pitch is how high or low a sound is.**

# Sound and hearing

Sound is produced when an object vibrates.
Think of ringing a bell.
The bell vibrates and makes the air around it vibrate.

bell
vibrates
air vibrates
ear
picks up
vibrations

We hear sound with our ears. They can pick up vibrations in the air. Nerves from the ear take messages to the brain. The brain then interprets these messages and tells us what might have made that sound.

**Without ears and brain we could not hear.**

### The ear

The ear has three main parts: the outer ear, the middle ear and the inner ear. The ear drum lies between the outer and middle ear.

1   The outer ear picks up sound waves travelling through the air. It directs them to the ear drum.

2   The ear drum is a piece of tightly stretched skin. It can vibrate (like a drum skin) at the speed of the vibrating air.

3   The middle ear has three small bones inside it. They carry the vibrations of the ear drum to the inner ear.

4   The inner ear contains a small bag, filled with liquid. The vibrations from the ear drum pass into the liquid. In the liquid are the ends of nerves. The nerves take the message of sound to the brain.

Below is a diagram of the ear.

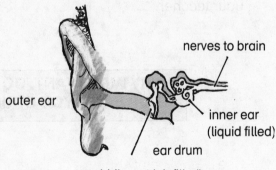

nerves to brain

outer ear

inner ear
(liquid filled)

ear drum

middle ear (air filled)

## Activities

1 How good are your ears? Can you recognise different sounds?

Get a friend to close his eyes. Make different sounds and ask your friend to guess what has caused these sounds.

Some ideas for making sounds are:

hitting a metal bucket
hitting a plastic bucket
clapping your hands
dropping a stick.

Think of some other ways of making sounds.

2 Get together with two or three friends and find out who can hear best. Make a fair way of finding out who is best. Discuss your method among yourselves and then with your teacher.

3 Can you imitate the sounds made by these birds?

a) cockerel

b) horned bill

**VERY IMPORTANT: DO NOT PUT THINGS INTO YOUR EARS. YOU COULD BADLY DAMAGE THEM.**

# How sound travels

## Activities

1   Take two small tins. Make a small hole in the bottom of each tin. Pass a string through both holes and tie a knot in each end of the string.

Hold one tin to your ear and get a friend to speak into the other tin. Pull the thread tight.

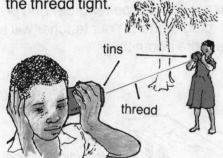

What can you hear?

2   In your school you may have a pipe attatched to the wall. Get a friend to tap on the pipe.
Put one end of a ruler on the pipe and hold the other end to your ear. What do you hear?

> **Remember, sound travels by vibrating the air.**
> **The vibrating air pushes on the still air next to it and makes that vibrate also.**
> **In this way the vibration is passed on.**

Activity 2, shows that sound can travel through solids. In fact, sound travels through solids, liquids and gases.

> **We say that sound travels in waves. Each wave is a small vibration of the air.**

Sound waves get weaker the further they are from the object making them. The school bell sounds very loud close to, but much less loud the further you move away from it.

# Echoes

Sound takes time to travel, although it travels very, very quickly.
When sound waves hit a hard object (like a wall) they bounce back. This is called reflection of sound. The reflected sound is called an echo.

**Activity**
Stand 100m or so from your school building or any wall. Clap your hands and listen to the echo. The time between your clap and the echo is the time it takes for the sound to go from you to the wall and back.

# Storing sound

Sound, like wheat, can be stored! You store wheat in a sack. Sound is stored on tapes of a special material. First the sound is recorded on the tape using a tape recorder machine. The sound is now 'in' the tape. You can store the tape for many years.
If you want to listen to the sound then you put it on a tape recorder and press the 'play' button. Your teacher will tell you more about this.

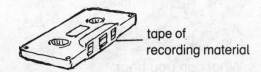

tape of
recording material

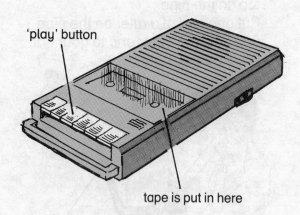

'play' button

tape is put in here

# 9 Respiration

All living things need to breathe. When you breathe, you take in fresh air through your nose or mouth. Your nose warms and filters the air (to remove dust). The warmed air travels down your windpipe and into your lungs.

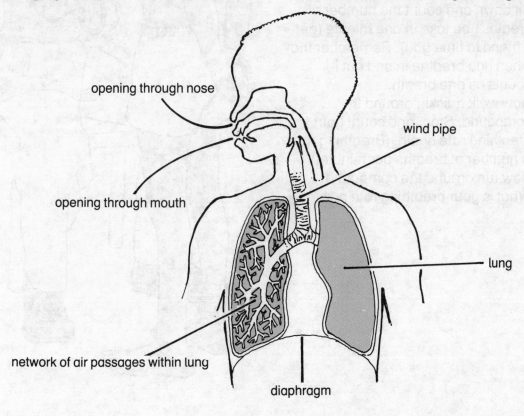

opening through nose

opening through mouth

wind pipe

lung

network of air passages within lung

diaphragm

In air there are several gases. <u>Oxygen</u> is one of these. It is vital for life. Oxygen is needed in all parts of your body. Without oxygen, cells die. Without air (and therefore oxygen), living things die.

## Activities

1   Ask a friend to breathe in and out. Watch his chest.
2   Put your hand on your chest. Breathe in and out. Feel your lungs filling with air.
3   Sit down and count the number of breaths you take in one minute (get a friend to time you). Remember that when you breathe in and out it counts as one breath.
4   Now walk quickly around the compound. Stop, and count your breathing rate again. (Breathing rate is number of breaths per minute.)
5   Now run around the compound. What is your breathing rate now?

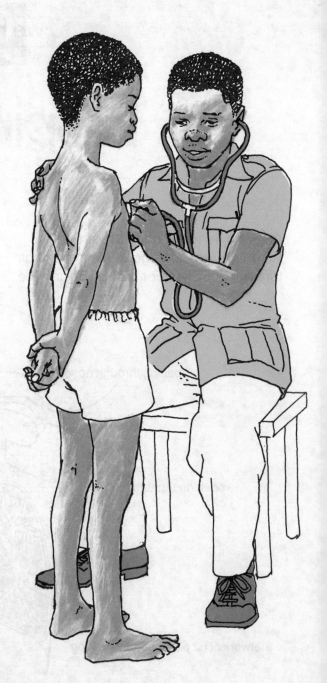

# How much oxygen do we need?

Our bodies need oxygen all the time, even when we are resting (sitting down for example).

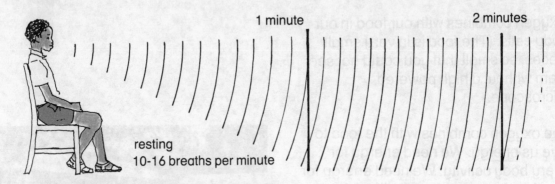

1 minute 2 minutes

resting
10-16 breaths per minute

We need more oxygen when we are walking.

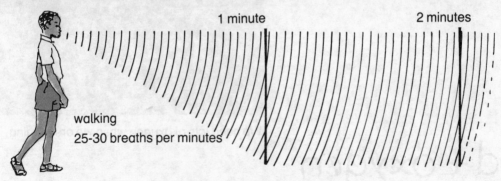

1 minute 2 minutes

walking
25-30 breaths per minutes

We need even more oxygen when we are running.

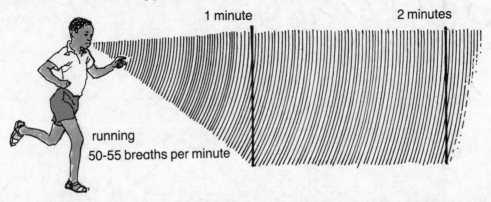

1 minute 2 minutes

running
50-55 breaths per minute

# Why do we need oxygen?

We have said that we need oxygen for life. Why is this?

Oxygen combines with our food in our body cells. (The food is in very small pieces, so small that you could not see them without a high powered microscope.)

The oxygen combines with the food to give us <u>energy</u>. We need energy for every body activity. We need energy for growing, for movement, for life.

We need lots of oxygen when we are running.

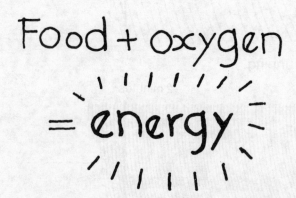

# How does oxygen get into the body?

Our lungs are full of air. How does air get into the lungs?

In the lungs are small air sacs. Oxygen goes from the air in the air sacs into very small blood vessels. The oxygen is carried in blood vessels to every cell in the body.

## Breathing in and out

When you breathe in, the bottom of your chest (the diaphragm) pushes down. The lungs get bigger and air is pulled into them.

**breathing in (inspiration)**

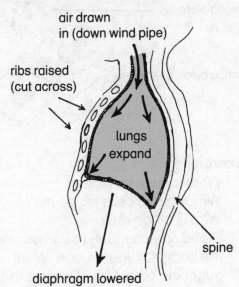

air drawn in (down wind pipe)

ribs raised (cut across)

lungs expand

diaphragm lowered

spine

When you breathe out, the diaphragm pushes up. The lungs get smaller and air is pushed out.

**breathing out (expiration)**

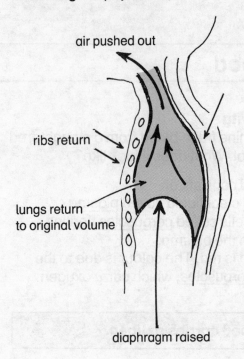

air pushed out

ribs return

lungs return to original volume

diaphragm raised

**Oxygen gets into our bodies through our lungs.**

# 10
# Blood circulation

## Blood

### Activity
Examine fresh blood from a slaughtered animal. What does it look like?

Blood consists of:
i)   a clear liquid called <u>plasma</u>
ii)  cells called <u>corpuscles</u> floating in the plasma.

Blood is red. The colour is due to the <u>red corpuscles</u>, which carry oxygen.

| **Blood carries oxygen.** |
| --- |

There are <u>white corpuscles</u> too. They protect the body against germs that cause disease.

If you look at blood through a miscroscope you can see these red and white cells. There are also tiny things called platelets. These help the blood to clot. What would happen if blood did not clot?

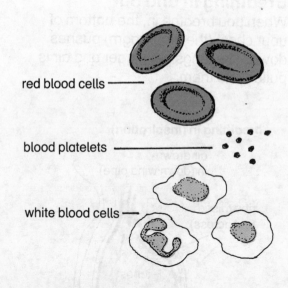

red blood cells ———

blood platelets ———

white blood cells ———

### Exercises
1   What makes up blood?
2   Which blood cells kill germs?
3   Why is blood red?
4   Blood carries many things around the body. Oxygen is one. What might the others be? Discuss this with your teacher.

# The heart

Where is your heart? What is its size and shape?

The heart is the pump of the body. What does it pump? What would happen if it stopped pumping?

The heart has four <u>chambers</u> or divisions – two on the left side and two on the right. The two halves of the heart are quite separate.

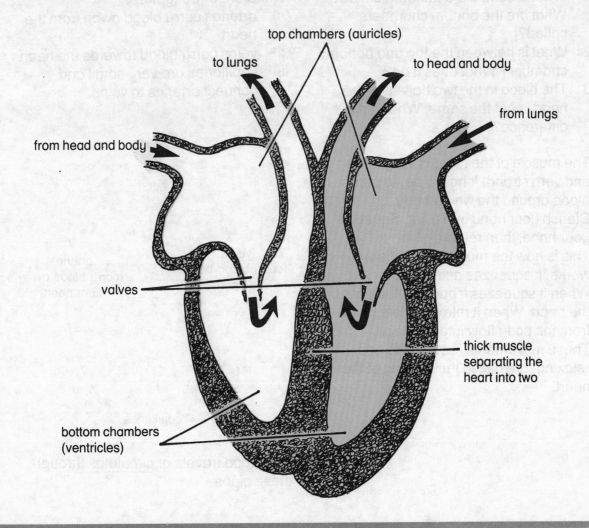

top chambers (auricles)

to lungs

to head and body

from lungs

from head and body

valves

thick muscle separating the heart into two

bottom chambers (ventricles)

## Activity

Visit your local market and look at a cow's heart which has been cut in half. What can you see?

A cow's heart is similar to a human heart.

## Exercises

Look at the drawing of the heart on page 77.

1   What are the top chambers called? What are the bottom chambers called?
2   What is between the top and bottom chamber? What does it do?
3   The blood in the two halves of the heart is not the same. What is the difference?

The muscle of the heart is very thick and very strong. It has to be, to pump blood around the whole body.
Clench your hand into a fist. Squeeze your hand, then relax it.
This is how the muscle in the heart works. It squeezes and relaxes.
When it squeezes it pumps blood out of the heart. When it relaxes it lets blood from the body flow into the heart.
These movements (squeezing and relaxing) are called the beating of the heart.

# Blood vessels

> **Blood is carried to all parts of the body in tubes called blood vessels.**

There are three types:
i)    arteries carry blood away from the heart
ii)   veins carry blood towards the heart
iii)  capillaries are very small and connect arteries to veins.

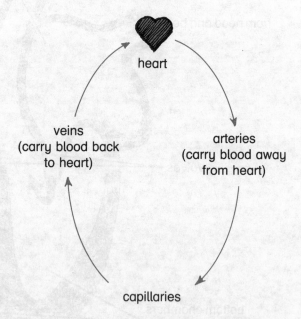

heart

veins
(carry blood back
to heart)

arteries
(carry blood away
from heart)

capillaries

The blood travels or circulates through these pipes.

## Activities

1  Your teacher will use a handkerchief to show you the veins on your arm. (These lie close to the surface of the skin so are easily seen.)
2  Examine a live frog or toad and look at its web. You teacher will help you.
3  Your teacher may bring in a freshly killed rabbit or other small animal. Look at the position and shape of its heart.
4  Place your ear on your neighbour's chest, on the left. What do you hear?

# How blood gets oxygen

Think back to your work on respiration. How does the blood get oxygen? It gets it from the lungs. Oxygen goes from the air in the air sacs into the blood.
What part of the blood carries oxygen?

The drawing shows the circulation of blood in the human body.

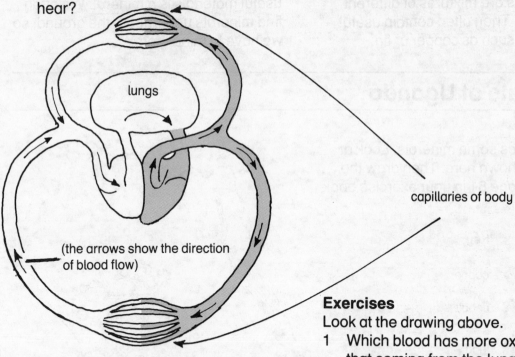

lungs

capillaries of body

(the arrows show the direction of blood flow)

5  Get your teacher to help you to locate pulse points on your body.
6  Make a stethoscope and listen to your friend's heart. Your teacher will help you to do this.

## Exercises

Look at the drawing above.
1  Which blood has more oxygen — that coming from the lungs or that going to the lungs?
2  The heart is divided down the middle. It has a right and a left half. Why is the heart divided? Discuss this with your teacher.

# 11

# Rocks and minerals

Collect some rocks and look at them. Most rocks are mixtures of different materials. They often contain useful materials such as copper or tin.

Another word for a rock containing useful materials is a <u>mineral</u>. We often find minerals underneath the ground, so we have to mine them.

## Minerals of Uganda

Uganda has some minerals. Look at the map shown here. Then draw the table on page 81 in your exercise book and fill it in.

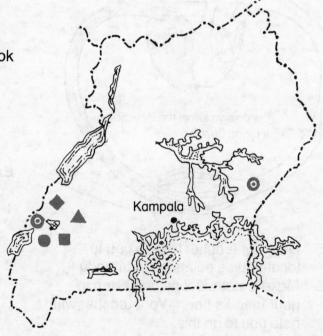

Key

◆ copper

▲ cobalt

● lead

■ zinc

◉ salt

Kampala

| minerals | place(s) where mineral is found |
|---|---|
|  |  |
|  |  |
|  |  |
|  |  |
|  |  |

Copper is the most important mineral in Uganda. It comes from the Kilembe mines near Fort Portal. It is dug from the Ruwenzori mountains and made pure at Jinja. Then it is sold to Japan and other countries.

Copper is a metal. A mineral containing copper is a metallic mineral or an <u>ore</u>. Other metallic minerals found in Uganda contain wolfram and tin.

Copper is used for making electric wires, kettles, boilers etc.

Wolfram (tungsten ore) is used for making the inside parts of electric light bulbs.

Tin is used for making baths and covering cans made of other metals.

Limestone is a non-metallic mineral. It is used for making cement. Cement is a powder made by heating limestone and clay together and grinding it up. It is used for building. Discuss with your teacher how cement is used.

**Activity**
Half-fill a cup with boiling water and add several large spoonfuls of rock salt. What happens to most of the salt?

Cool a lttle and pour into a glass. (Do not pour boiling water directly into the glass.)
Now hang a piece of string over the glass so that the end dips in the water. Do not move the string for about three weeks. What happens to the string?

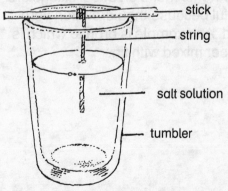

You should find that <u>crystals</u> of salt form on the string. Many minerals are made from crystals. What do the salt crystals look like?

# Metals

Many of the things around us are made of metal. Metals are usually hard and strong and often shiny. They are very useful to us.

Metals are often found in the rocks of the earth (usually mixed with other things). They have to be mined. Rocks containing metals are called ores.

Some metals are found pure in the ground. They are not mixed with anything else. Gold, silver and mercury are found pure. Other metals are impure and are mixed with other things. Often it is quite hard to separate the metal and make it pure.

We often mix several pure metals together to make an alloy. Alloys are useful because they are often very hard. An example is bronze which is copper mixed with tin.

## Activities

1   Make a list of fifteen different objects in your classroom. Group them into metals or non-metals. Many objects will be made of metal and non-metal. Put these in a third group.
2   Discuss these with your teacher:
    i)   How is metal different from wood or cloth?
    ii)  Why is it bad to throw metals away in the compound?
    iii) How many useful things can you think of that are made of metal?
3   Go outside and collect different kinds of metal that have been thrown away. Look for others that are being used.

# Describing metals and their uses

Look at the metals that you have collected from Activity 3. Try to identify them using this chart.

| | | |
|---|---|---|
| **copper** | A red brown metal. It is soft and can be hammered and beaten into shapes. It is often found in lumps. | Pure copper allows electricity to pass through it very easily. It is used to make all sorts of wires. Copper is a very good conductor of heat. |
| **iron** | A shiny metal which goes rusty. It is also dark and silvery. It is easily pulled by a magnet. | Nails, knives and many tools are made of iron. Heat passes through it easily. |
| **aluminium** | A shiny metal, but can also be dull (covered with a white powder). It is light and strong. It is common in the rocks of the earth. | Used for making saucepans and all sorts of cooking pots. Used in the building of aircrafts. |
| **lead** | A soft grey metal. When scratched, it looks like silver. | It is used in making water pipes and car batteries. |
| **zinc** | A grey metal. Crystals usually easily visible on the surface. | It is used for covering things made of iron, e.g. corrugated iron sheets and wires for fencing etc. |
| **tin** | A shiny soft metal. | It is used for covering cans made of iron. |
| **chromium** | A very shiny metal. | Very shiny parts on cars e.g. bumpers or headlamp reflectors are covered with a thin layer of chromium. |
| **gold** | A soft yellow metal which is very dense. It can be hammered and beaten into many shapes. | Used for making sports medals and jewellery. |

## Activities

1  Look at five and ten cent coins. How do they feel? What are they made of?

2  Examine razor blades and spoons. What are they made of?

## Mixtures of metals

We have already talked about alloys. These are mixtures of metals. They are often stronger than pure metals and are cheaper.

Look at the pictures below and fill in the table.

these are made of bronze
(copper and tin)

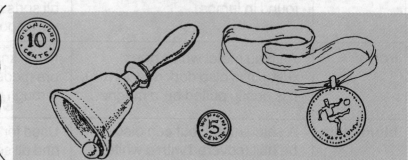

these are made of steel
(iron and carbon)

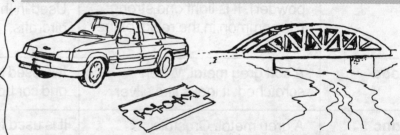

taps are often brass
(copper and zinc)

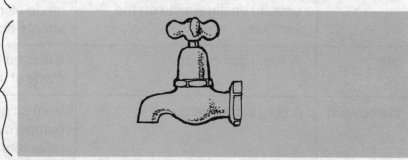

| alloy | made from | uses |
|-------|-----------|------|
| steel | iron and carbon | |
| bronze | copper and tin | |
| brass | copper and zinc | |

**Exercises**

1 Make a list of things made of:
   i)   iron
   ii)   copper
   iii)  aluminium
   iv)  gold.

2 Why are zinc and tin used to cover iron objects? Discuss this with your teacher.

3 Make a list of things made of bronze, steel and brass.

4 List ten things in your home made of metal.

5 What is an alloy? Why are alloys useful?

6 Discuss with your teacher how iron is got (extracted) from the ground.

**Metals are extracted from mineral ores.**
**Metals are crystals.**
**Alloys are mixtures of metals.**

# 12

# Magnetism

## Activities

1    Collect objects such as pens, pins, matches, nails, pencils, clips, rubbers, plastic pencil sharpeners and coins.
Your teacher will give you a <u>magnet</u>. It is made from a magnetic substance.

Try to pick up each object with the magnet.
Make a table, like the one shown below, in your exercise book.
Fill it in.

| Materials picked up by a magnet | Materials not picked up by a magnet |
|---|---|
|  |  |
|  |  |
|  |  |
|  |  |
|  |  |
| These a called magnetic substances. | These are called non-magnetic substances. |

**Some substances are <u>attracted</u> to magnets. They are called <u>magnetic</u> substances.**

2   Place your magnet underneath a sheet of paper sprinkled with iron filings or drawing pins.
    Where do most of the filings or pins gather?

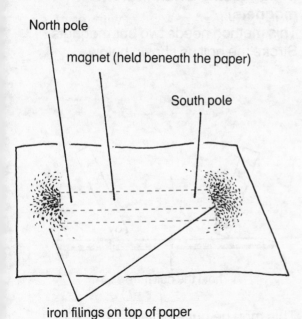

North pole

magnet (held beneath the paper)

South pole

iron filings on top of paper

The ends of the magnets are called poles. There is a North pole and a South pole. A long magnet like the ones drawn here is called a bar <u>magnet</u>.

3   Make a stand from wood. Hang a magnet by a string from the stand.

Let it swing until it stands perfectly still. Which direction is it pointing? Repeat the experiment. Does it come to rest in a different position?

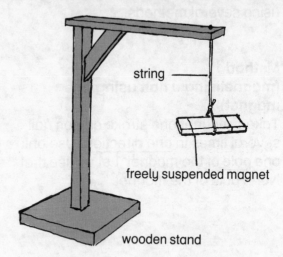

string

freely suspended magnet

wooden stand

4   Use two stands this time. To each stand tie a magnet as before.

Push the two stands closer until the magnets are nearly touching. What happens?

We say that two South poles are <u>like</u> poles. (They are the same.) A North and a South pole are <u>unlike</u> poles. (They are different.)

Now turn one of the magnets the other way around.

Again, push the magnets close together. What happens? What can you say about like poles and unlike poles.

# Making a magnet

Here is how to make your own magnet using several methods.

## Method 1
### (magnetising a nail using one magnet)

Take a magnet and stroke an iron nail several times in <u>one direction</u>. Use only <u>one pole</u> of the magnet. Let us use the North pole of the magnet.

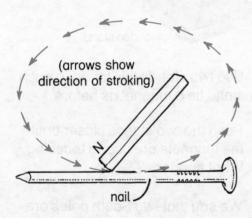

(arrows show direction of stroking)

nail

Now suspend the nail and the magnet from the wooden stands.
Is the head of the nail a North pole or a South pole? How can you tell?
What about the other end of the nail?
Discuss these results with your teacher.
Try stroking the nail in the <u>opposite direction</u>. Is the head of the nail a North or a South pole?

Now repeat the experiment but stroke the nail with the South pole of the magnet.
Again, suspend the nail and magnet. Which end is the North pole now?

## Method 2
### (magnetising a nail with two magnets)

This method needs two bar magnets. Stroke the nail as shown below.

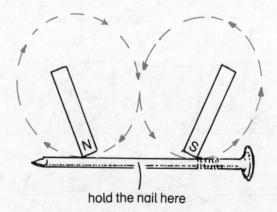

hold the nail here

This may be quite difficult to do. Get a friend to hold the nail to a table while you stroke with the magnets. You will need quite a long nail.
Now test the ends of the nail as you did for Method 1. Instead of magnets, try using the magnetised nails from Method 1. (You must remember where the poles are on these nails.)
Discuss your results with your teacher.

## Method 3
### (magnetising a nail by induction)

Put some small iron nails or office pins on one pole of a magnet.
What happens when you lift the magnet?
Now see if you can make a magnetic chain as shown below.
How many nails can you build into your chain?

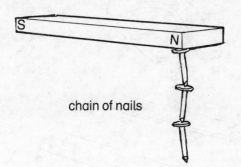

chain of nails

Each nail has been made into a small magnet.

Now put some small nails on the North pole of a bar magnet and leave them for an hour. Then remove the magnet and lay the nails out on the desk top. Bring the nails close to each other.
What happens?
What has happened to the nails?

## Method 4
### (magnetising an iron nail by electricity or electromagnetism)

Coil an insulated copper wire neatly around a nail. Connect the ends of the wire to a battery.

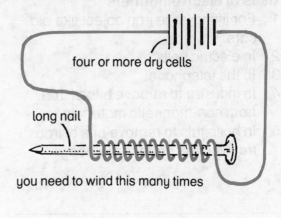

four or more dry cells

long nail

you need to wind this many times

The battery supplies an electric current which flows in the wire.
Bring some of the magnetised small nails near to the nail while the current is flowing.

Are they attracted to the large nail?
Is the nail still magnetised when the current is switched off?

A magnet produced by an electric current is called an electromagnet. It is only a magnet while the current flows.

## Uses of electromagnets

1   For lifting large iron object like old cars.
2   In electric bells.
3   In the telephone.
4   In industry to remove bits of iron from non-magnetic materials.
5   In hospitals to remove bits of iron from injured parts of the body.

# Temporary and permanent magnets

The type of magnets which you have made are called temporary magnets. They do not stay magnetised for long.

Permanent magnets are mostly made of alloys e.g. steel. They do not lose their magnetism easily. It is possible to destroy the magnetism of a permanent magnet by heating it until it is red hot. Hammering, also, makes it lose its magnetism.

# What makes a magnet?

Magnets are made of magnetic materials called ferromagnetic materials. These are iron, steel, cobalt and nickel.
Magnets come in all shapes and sizes. Some examples are shown here.

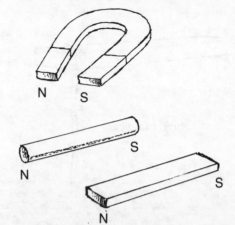

If like poles of two magnets are brought close together, they repel each other.

If unlike poles are brought close together they attract each other.

We can make magnets by stroking, induction and electricity.

If magnets are treated roughly or heated they can lose their magnetism. They are demagnetised.

## How does an iron nail become magnetised?

An iron nail is made of unmagnetised magnetic material. The particles are arranged in a <u>random</u> order.

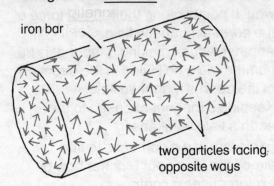

iron bar

two particles facing opposite ways

On magnetising the nail, the particles are arranged to face the same way.

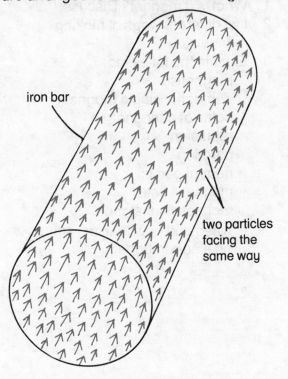

iron bar

two particles facing the same way

# Magnetic fields

> **A magnet exerts a force which we call magnetism.**

It is this magnetic force which makes unlike poles come together and like poles repel each other.

> **The space around a magnet where this force is felt is called its field of force or its <u>magnetic field</u>.**

### Activities

1   Place a bar magnet on a table and cover it with a sheet of paper. Sprinkle iron filings on the paper and tap it gently. Observe what happens. The lines made by the iron filings show the lines of magnetic force.

Record the pattern made by the iron filings.
Repeat the experiment.
Does the same pattern form?

2   Arrange two bar magnets in four different ways, as shown in the diagram below.

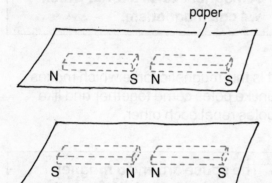

paper

Cover the magnets in each case with a piece of paper. Sprinkle iron filings on the paper and gently tap. Record the patterns made by the iron filings.

The areas where the iron filings do not collect are known as <u>neutral points</u>.

## Magnetic field of the earth

The earth is like a large magnet. It has a North pole and a South pole.

When a magnet is freely suspended it always comes to rest facing the same way. It points along the lines of force of the earth's magnetic field.

Another way of making a magnet is by hammering a nail lying in the direction of the earth's magnetic field.

Keeping a magnet exposed to the earth's field weakens it.

Explorers use a compass to find directions. Ask your teacher how an explorer uses a compass.

### Exercises
1   What is a magnet? Discuss.
2   List different ways of making magnets.
3   Explain the following:
    magnetism
    demagnetising a magnet
    poles of a magnet
    repulsion
    attration
    neutral points
    magnetic field
    magnetic substance
    when and how to use a compass
    an electromagnet.